MW00965377

Mummies!
Unwrapping the Secrets
of Ancient Egypt

by
Helen Sillett

Don Johnston Incorporated
Volo, Illinois

Edited by:

John Bergez
Start-to-Finish Core Content Series Editor, Pacifica, California

Alan Venable, MA
Start-to-Finish Core Content Developmental Editor, San Francisco, California

Gail Portnuff Venable, MS, CCC-SLP
Speech/Language Pathologist, San Francisco, California

Dorothy Tyack, MA
Learning Disabilities Specialist, San Francisco, California

Jerry Stemach, MS, CCC-SLP
Speech/Language Pathologist, Director of Content Development, Sonoma County, California

Graphics and Illustrations:

Photographs and illustrations are all created professionally
and modified to provide the best possible support for the
intended reader.
Cover image: © Thomas Hartwell/CORBIS
Page 37: MediaFocus International, LLC and/or its suppliers
All other photos © Don Johnston Incorporated and its licensors.

Narration:

Professional actors and actresses read the text to build
excitement and to model research-based elements of fluency:
intonation, stress, prosody, phrase groupings and rate.
The rate has been set to maximize comprehension for the reader.

Published by:

Don Johnston Incorporated
26799 West Commerce Drive
Volo, IL 60073

800.999.4660 USA Canada
800.889.5242 Technical Support
www.donjohnston.com

International Standard Book Number
ISBN 1-4105-0409-3

Contents

Getting Started

What do you think this is?

Take a look at this picture. Try to guess what it is before you read more.

You are looking at a picture of a **mummy** from the land of ancient Egypt. A mummy is a dead body that has been prepared so that it will last for many years. A mummy will not rot or fall apart as fast as other dead bodies. Egyptians began making mummies about 5000 years ago.

How did the Egyptians make a dead body into a mummy? Most often, the first step was to take the brain, lungs, and other inside parts out of the body. Next, the body was dried out. Then it was rubbed with a special oil, and it was wrapped in long strips of cloth.

Why did the ancient Egyptians make mummies? That's a good question to ask an **archeologist**. An archeologist is a scientist who studies the things that ancient people have left behind. Archeologists say the Egyptians believed that dead people could go on living after death. Dead people could live forever in a world that was called the **afterlife**. But they could only live in the afterlife as long as their bodies were safe and in good shape. If the body rotted or fell apart, the dead person would die forever.

The Egyptians had to protect the mummies so they wouldn't be stolen or damaged. One way to protect the mummy was by putting it in a tomb. A tomb is a room or building where a dead body is kept.

Maybe you've heard about the pyramids of ancient Egypt. The ancient Egyptians built the pyramids as tombs for their kings. The kings were called pharaohs. When a pharaoh died, the Egyptian priests would make his body into a mummy. Then the mummy was put in a tomb along with all the things that he might want in the afterlife.

This book is about mummies. It's also about the ideas that the ancient Egyptians had about the afterlife. You'll learn why they turned cats and crocodiles into mummies. You'll find out about the things that the Egyptians wanted to take with them into the afterlife.

You'll read about robbers who tried to steal gold from the tombs and how the Egyptians tried to stop them. And you'll see what archeologists have found inside mummies.

Article 1

Food and Servants
for the Dead

Questions this article will answer:

• **Why did the ancient Egyptians give food to the dead?**

• **Why did the ancient Egyptians make food mummies?**

• **Why did the pharaoh need servants after he died?**

This is a picture of an ancient Egyptian grave. As you can see, it's not a fancy grave. The naked body was just put into a hole, and the ground was so dry that the body dried out before it could rot.

This man was buried in the desert more than 5000 years ago.

You can see some small pots next to the body. Take a guess about what these pots were for.

Why do you think they were put into the grave?

Someone put these pots into the grave for the dead man to use in the afterlife. In this article, you'll read more about the things that the Egyptians wanted to have in the afterlife.

Food for the Dead

To stay alive, people need food. The ancient Egyptians believed that a dead person needed food, too.

This picture is from the wall of an ancient Egyptian tomb. It shows Egyptians collecting food.

They put food in graves and tombs so that the dead person wouldn't be hungry after death.

Archeologists have found many different kinds of food in ancient Egyptian tombs and graves. Sometimes, the food is raw. For example, archeologists have found large stone jars filled with grain. The ancient Egyptians must have thought that the dead person could grind the grain into flour and then use the flour to bake bread.

Food from an ancient Egyptian tomb

Sometimes, the Egyptians cooked the food before they put it in the tomb so that the dead person would have something to eat right away. In one grave, archeologists found a set of bowls full of food. The food was a feast for the dead person — a feast of fish, beef, cake, fruit, and cheese.

Archeologists have also found food in stone boxes. The outsides of the boxes were carved with pictures to show what was inside. They were pictures of cakes, bread, and meat.

Food Mummies

The pharaoh was buried with animals and meat that had been made into food mummies. Food mummies would last a long time without rotting. One of the ancient pharaohs was called Tutankhamun or King Tut.

These are pictures of some of the things that were found in King Tut's tomb. Here you see a board game and gold-covered statues of a man and a jackal.

His tomb had more than 40 boxes of food mummies in it.

Most people couldn't afford to have food mummies made for their tombs or graves. But the pharaoh was rich and important, so he ordered his servants to fill his tomb with everything that he would want in the afterlife.

This model of a boat and these small blue statues were found in King Tut's tomb. They were supposed to help take him to the afterlife.

Here is how food mummies were made. Large animals like cows and goats were cut into pieces. These pieces looked a lot like the meat that you buy in a grocery store today. Chickens, ducks, and other small animals were not cut into pieces, but their heads and feet were cut off.

The meat was usually covered in salt because salt would dry it out. Drying the meat helped to preserve it, just like a piece of beef jerky. After the meat was preserved, it was wrapped in strips of cloth, just like a human mummy. Then the food mummy was put inside a wooden box or coffin.

Sometimes, the food mummy was soaked in oil. Why? Archeologists think that it was soaked in oil to get it ready to be cooked in the afterlife.

Servants for the Pharaoh

A living pharaoh had many servants to take care of him. The ancient Egyptians believed that the pharaoh would also need servants in the afterlife.

Early in the history of ancient Egypt, the pharaoh may have gone into the afterlife with real human servants. About 5000 years ago, archeologists think that some of a pharaoh's servants were put to death when the pharaoh died. They were killed so that they could serve him in the afterlife. The graves of servants were dug near the pharaoh's tomb.

Archeologists think that the killing of servants stopped about 4600 years ago, when the ancient Egyptians started to believe that pictures or statues of servants could take care of the dead pharaoh instead of the servants themselves. Maybe the servants came up with this idea! Artists painted or carved pictures of servants on the walls of the pharaoh's tomb. These pictures showed servants who were feeding animals or farming or doing other jobs for the pharaoh.

Some tombs contain statues of servants. These statues were carved out of stone. They show the servants doing things like grinding corn, baking bread, and even making beer.

A statue of a woman who is grinding wheat to make flour

Summary

In this article, you read about some things that the ancient Egyptians wanted to have in the afterlife. One thing was food. Food mummies were made for the tombs of the pharaohs. Ancient Egyptian pharaohs also wanted servants to work for them in the afterlife.

Article 2

Animal Mummies

Questions this article will answer:

- How did the ancient Egyptians make cat mummies?

- Why did the ancient Egyptians make cat mummies?

- Why did some ancient Egyptians make their pets into mummies?

Look at this picture. This is a cat mummy. Archeologists have discovered thousands of mummies like this one in Egypt. Archeologists think that the Egyptians made more than a million cat mummies. Many of them were found buried together in large graves.

A cat mummy

The ancient Egyptians also made other kinds of animal mummies. Archeologists have found mummies of bulls, snakes, crocodiles, falcons, and many other animals.

How did the Egyptians make animals into mummies? And why did they bother to do it? To answer these questions, let's talk about cats.

How to Make a Cat Mummy

Let's look at how the ancient Egyptians made cat mummies. There were four things they often did to the dead cat: clean it out, dry it, stuff it, and wrap it.

Sometimes, the first step in making a cat mummy was to cut open the cat's body and take out its heart and lungs, stomach, and other inside parts. These parts of a body are called the internal organs.

After the internal organs were taken out, they were thrown away. Or sometimes, the internal organs were left inside the cat.

The second step was to dry out the cat's body. The ancient Egyptians dried out the body by covering it with a powder called natron. Natron is a kind of salt that the Egyptians found in the desert. The natron helped to pull the water out of the cat's body. If the internal organs were taken out, step three was to stuff the cat's body with sand or mud. The last step was to wrap the body in strips of cloth.

Sometimes, the Egyptians put a mask that looked like a head on top of the cat mummy. The mask was made from cloth and plaster. Sometimes, the mummy was put inside a coffin that was shaped like a cat.

Some cat mummies were put inside stone coffins like this one.

Animal Mummies and Religion

Cats were a part of the religion of ancient Egypt. This is the main reason that they were made into mummies.

Other animals were also part of the Egyptian religion. The Egyptians believed in many gods, and they worshipped different gods in different ways. They made pictures of some of the gods as animals. One god was often shown as a baboon, and another as a crocodile. About 2900 years ago, the Egyptians began to believe that the spirits of gods and goddesses lived inside the bodies of animals. For example, the ancient Egyptians had a goddess who was called Bastet. They believed that the spirit of Bastet lived on earth in a holy cat.

A **pilgrim** is a person who travels a long way to visit a holy place. Pilgrims came from all over Egypt to worship the holy cat in the temple of Bastet. Archeologists believe that many cat mummies were made as gifts for Bastet.

People who lived near the temple made the cat mummies and then sold them to the pilgrims. Then the pilgrims took the mummies to the temple of Bastet. We call these cat mummies **votive mummies**. The word "votive" means something that people give as an offering as a part of worship. For example, in some churches today, people burn votive candles as a way to worship or pray to God. Archeologists have found thousands of these votive cat mummies. They were buried in giant pits near the ruins of Bastet's temple. In that part of ancient Egypt, there was probably never a problem with stray cats!

Cat mummies weren't the only votive mummies. The Egyptians made votive mummies of many different kinds of animals. They may have made millions of them. Archeologists have discovered huge graves and tombs filled with animal mummies from floor to ceiling — crocodiles, baboons, falcons, rams, and others.

A crocodile mummy

Pet Mummies

Not all animal mummies were votive mummies. Some animals were pets that were made into mummies so that they could follow their owners around in the afterlife.

Archeologists have found some **pet mummies** right in the tombs of their owners. One of these tombs was the tomb of a man named Hapy-Min. A mummy of Hapy-Min's pet dog was found at his feet in the tomb.

Some pet mummies had their own tombs. One king had a special tomb and coffin built for his guard dog named Abutiu. The son of another king had his cat buried in a large stone coffin that looked just like the coffin of a wealthy human.

Ancient Egyptian art is full of pictures of animals, and many pictures of pets and other animals have been found on the walls of ancient Egyptian tombs. The art and the pet mummies show that the ancient Egyptians loved animals.

Summary

In this article, you read about different kinds of animal mummies. You learned how the Egyptians made cat mummies. Votive animal mummies were part of ancient Egyptian religion. These mummies were given as gifts to the gods. Some ancient Egyptians made their pets into mummies so they could take them into the afterlife.

Article 3

Robbing Tombs

Questions this article will answer:

- **What did the ancient Egyptians do to keep robbers from finding the pharaohs' tombs?**

- **How did the ancient Egyptians try to scare robbers away from tombs?**

In 1922, an ancient tomb was discovered by a man named Howard Carter, an archeologist from England. It was the tomb of a young pharaoh called Tutankhamun or King Tut. King Tut's tomb was filled from floor to ceiling with treasures. One was the solid gold coffin of the pharaoh Tutankhamun himself.

The inside of King Tut's tomb
when it was discovered in 1922.

Howard Carter had made a great discovery. Other tombs of the pharaohs had been found by archeologists, but they had all been empty when the archeologists opened them. The tombs had been robbed in ancient times, and the robbers had taken the treasures.

The pharaohs didn't want their tombs to be robbed. The things in the tomb were all meant to go with the pharaoh into the afterlife. If they were stolen, the pharaoh's mummy would not be able to use them. It would be like going on a trip and losing all of your luggage.

Let's see how the ancient Egyptians tried to stop the robbers.

Tricks to Stop Robbers

The ancient Egyptians used many tricks to keep the robbers from finding and stealing treasures from the tombs. Let's look at a pyramid that is called the Great Pyramid to learn more about these tricks.

The Great Pyramid

One way to protect the mummy and the treasures was to hide the entrance to the pyramid.

This is the entrance to the Great Pyramid. In ancient times, the entrance was hidden.

First, the pharaoh's mummy was put inside a room inside the pyramid. Archeologists call this kind of room a **burial chamber**. The treasure was also put in chambers inside the pyramid.

34

Then the outside of the pyramid was covered with smooth pieces of limestone. To finish the job, the entrance to the pyramid was also covered with limestone so that the robbers would not know how to get in.

The pyramid builders had other ways to make it hard for robbers to find the chambers, too. They didn't make just one tunnel that led straight to the chambers. Instead, they made a maze of tunnels so that the robbers would get lost inside the pyramid. Some of the long tunnels were dead ends that didn't lead to anything.

Sometimes, the builders made a secret hole in the roof of a tunnel. These secret holes would lead to the burial chamber. The builders hoped that the robbers would never find the hole, and so they would never reach the burial chamber. The hole in the roof of the tunnel was hidden by a giant, flat rock.

35

The builders also used big, heavy stones or piles of rocks to block the entrance to the burial chamber. This was supposed to keep the robbers from getting into the chamber, even if they knew where it was.

Most of these tricks didn't work. Even with all the dead-end tunnels and secret doors, the robbers still found their way to the burial chambers to steal the mummies and treasures.

Curses Inside the Tombs

The Egyptians had another way to try to keep robbers from stealing from tombs — they wrote **curses** inside the tombs. The curses warned the robbers about all the bad things that would happen to them if they stole from the tomb. The robbers were supposed to be scared away by the curses.

Curses were not used very much in the tombs of the pharaohs. Archeologists have found the curses mainly in the tombs of ordinary Egyptians.

One ancient curse warned the robber that snakes and crocodiles would attack him if he stole anything from the tomb.

One curse warned robbers that crocodiles might attack them if they stole from a tomb.

"A crocodile will eat him in the water.

Or a snake will bite him on land.

This will happen to anyone who does anything against this tomb."

Another curse warns the robber not to steal from the tomb, or else his own things may be stolen.

"Anything that you do against this tomb of mine will mean trouble for you. The same thing will happen to things that you own."

The same curse sends another warning to a robber who enters the tomb.

"If any person enters my tomb, I will grab him like a goose! I will make him fear the sight of ghosts upon the earth."

Archeologists have found another curse that they call "the donkey curse." The donkey curse was used to protect buildings or land that had been given to someone in a will. When you make a will, you write down who you want to have your things after you die.

The god Seth was shown as a donkey in pictures. The donkey curse said that, if people did not obey someone's will, they would be attacked by a donkey!

Summary

In this article, you read about trying to keep robbers from stealing from tombs. The pyramids were filled with tricks to fool robbers, but most of the tricks didn't work. Some ordinary Egyptians used curses to try to keep robbers away. Probably, these curses didn't work either if there was something good to steal.

Article 4

Looking Inside Mummies

Questions this article will answer:

- In 1981, scientists got the chance to unwrap a human mummy. What did they find inside?

- What did the scientists find out about the mummy's brain?

- How do scientists look inside cat mummies these days?

Look at this picture of a human mummy from ancient Egypt. You can see that the mummy is wrapped in long strips of cloth.

A mummy in the British Museum

In 1981, a team of scientists in England unwrapped an Egyptian mummy like this one. It was the mummy of an ancient Egyptian priest named Horemkenesi. The scientists wanted to study the mummy carefully to see what they could learn about ancient Egypt and the priest.

You may be surprised by some of the shocking things that the scientists discovered by unwrapping the mummy.

41

You may also be surprised by the things that scientists have found inside cat mummies.

Unwrapping a Human Mummy

It was exciting for the scientists to get to unwrap a mummy in 1981, because they didn't get to do this very often. Unwrapping usually destroyed the mummies, and scientists had realized that it was important to protect them.

In the old days, people had not worried much about destroying mummies. In the old days, explorers brought mummies back to Europe and held parties where they unwrapped them. They invited their guests to watch. They served food and drinks to the guests. They unwrapped the mummies quickly, and they didn't study them very carefully.

In 1981, the scientists unwrapped the mummy of the priest Horemkenesi slowly and carefully. They took pictures of the work, made a video, and took notes about everything that they saw. They took two weeks to finish the job. This wasn't anything like the mummy parties of the explorers.

What did the scientists find under all those strips of cloth? One thing they found was lots of bugs. The inside layers of cloth were full of beetles. Priest Horemkenesi's face and neck were full of holes. The beetles had made these holes by eating through Horemkenesi's skin.

Horemkenesi's eyeballs were still in his head. But they were not round any more. They had lost their round shape, and they had sunk into the back of his eye sockets. The head also still had teeth, but the teeth were yellow and loose.

The scientists could see that Horemkenesi's head had been shaved. Most ancient Egyptian priests had shaved heads. There was some stubble of hair on his head and chin. From the stubble, the scientists knew that Horemkenesi had black hair with some grey and white hairs mixed in.

Horemkenesi's Brain

The beetles had eaten more than skin. The scientists were surprised to see that the beetles had also eaten Horemkenesi's brain. Why was this such a big surprise?

The scientists were surprised because, in most human mummies from Egypt, the brain was taken out of the skull before the body was wrapped in cloth.

Usually, the Egyptians pulled out the brain, bit by bit, through the nose. They pushed a thin, metal rod up the dead person's nose until the rod broke through the bone behind the nose. The rod made a hole that reached into the skull. Then the brain was pulled out through the hole.

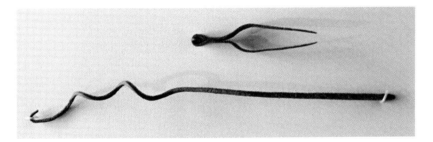

A tool that was used to pull out a
dead person's brain through his nose

The scientists could see that the Egyptians had not taken Horemkenesi's brain out through the nose. Behind the nose, the bone had not been broken.

The Egyptians had made Horemkenesi into a mummy with his brain still inside his skull.

After Horemkenesi was made into a mummy and was buried, beetles took over his body. The beetles ate their way into his skull, and then they ate his brain. So when the scientists looked inside his skull, they found no brain at all. Instead, they found dead beetles.

This is the kind of beetle that attacked Horemkenesi's mummy.

Inside the Cat Mummies

Archeologists have discovered some amazing things by looking inside cat mummies. How do they look inside the mummies?

They use X-rays. With X-rays, archeologists can study the insides of a mummy without hurting it.

Look at this picture of a cat mummy. At the British Museum, scientists X-rayed this mummy to see what was inside it. They discovered something very strange. This mummy was big enough to contain a large adult cat, but the X-ray showed that the mummy contained the body of a kitten that was maybe three or four months old when it died.

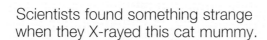

Scientists found something strange when they X-rayed this cat mummy.

There was another strange thing about this cat mummy. The head of an adult cat was stuck onto the body of the kitten. We don't know why the Egyptians did this.

The X-rays of other cat mummies show that many of the mummies were kittens. Some of the X-rays show that the kittens had been killed. Many of them had their necks broken. Others had their skulls bashed in.

Why were these kittens killed? Archeologists think they know. They think the Egyptians sold the cat mummies to people who wanted to give gifts to the goddess Bastet because her spirit lived in cats. The Egyptians probably raised cats to make them into mummies for the goddess. Maybe they used kittens when they ran out of full-grown cats.

Summary

In this article, you read about the insides of human and cat mummies. In 1981, scientists unwrapped the mummy of a priest called Horemkenesi. Instead of a brain, they found dead beetles that had eaten the brain. Today, scientists use X-ray machines to look inside mummies, and inside large cat mummies, they have found kittens instead of full-grown cats.

Glossary

Word	Definition	Page
afterlife	In ancient Egypt, people believed that they would go to another world after they died. This was called the afterlife.	5
archeologist	a scientist who studies the things that ancient people have left behind	5
burial chamber	In ancient Egypt, a room where a **mummy** was buried was called a burial chamber.	34
cat mummies	bodies of dead cats that were prepared and wrapped up so that they would last for a long time	21
curses	warnings about all the bad things that would happen to robbers if they stole things from **tombs**	36
food mummies	food that was prepared and wrapped up so that it would last for a long time	13
internal organs	the heart, lungs, and other organs that are inside a body	22

Word	Definition	Page
mummy	a dead body that was prepared and wrapped up so that it would last for many years	4
natron	a kind of salt that was used to dry out dead bodies before they were turned into **mummies**	23
pet mummies	bodies of pets that were prepared and wrapped up so that they would last for a long time	28
pharaohs	the kings of ancient Egypt	6
pilgrim	a person who travels a long way to visit a holy place	25
pyramids	giant **tombs** where some of the kings of ancient Egypt were buried	6
tomb	a room or a building where a dead body is buried	6
votive mummies	**mummies** that were given to one of the gods as a part of worship	26

About the Author

Helen Sillett was born in England and lived in the Netherlands and Canada before moving to California as a teenager. She has taught history and literature classes to college students, and reading and writing classes to young adults. She is a writer and editor and has been a member of the Start-to-Finish team for several years.

Helen has loved animals and the outdoors since she was a child. She spends many hours chasing after her dog, Ella, on the hiking trails near their home in Los Angeles.

About the Narrator

Nick Sandys has performed on stage in theaters in Chicago, New York, Dallas, London, England, and Edinburgh, Scotland. You may also have heard Nick's voice in a television or radio commercial.

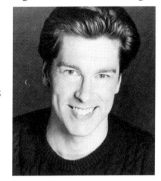

Nick is a member of Actors' Equity Association, the Screen Actors Guild, and AFTRA and is a certified fight director with the Society of American Fight Directors. Nick has an MA in English Literature and is working on a PhD. He grew up in the ancient city of York, in the north of England.

A Note to the Teacher

Start-to-Finish Core Content books are designed to help students achieve success in reading to learn. From the provocative cover question to the carefully structured and considerate text, these books promote inquiry, active engagement, and understanding. Not only do students learn curriculum-relevant content, but they learn how to read with understanding. Here are some of the features that make these books such powerful aids in teaching and learning.

Structure That Supports Inquiry and Understanding

Core Content books are carefully structured to encourage students to ask questions, identify main ideas, and understand how ideas relate to one another. The structural features of the Gold Core Content books include the following:

- **"Getting Started"**: A concise introduction engages students in the book's topic and explicitly states what they will learn.
- **Clearly focused articles:** Each of the following articles focuses on a single topic at a length that makes for a comfortable session of reading.
- **"Questions This Article Will Answer"**: Provocative questions following the article title reflect the article's main ideas. Each question corresponds to a heading within the article.
- **Article introduction:** An engaging opening leads to a clear statement of the article topic.
- **Carefully worded headings:** The headings within each article are carefully worded to signal the main idea of the section and reflect the opening questions.
- **Clear topic statements:** Within each article section, the main idea is explicitly stated so that students can distinguish it from supporting details.
- **"Summary"**: A brief Summary in each article recaptures the main ideas signaled by the opening questions, text headings, and topic statements.

Text That Is Written for Success™

Every page of a Core Content book is the product of a skilled team of educators, writers, and editors who understand your students' needs. The text features of these books include the following:

- **Mature treatment of grade level curriculum:** Core Content is age and grade-appropriate for the older student who is actively acquiring reading skills. The books also contain information that may be new to any student in the class, empowering Core Content readers to contribute interesting information to class discussions.
- **Idioms and vocabulary:** The text limits the density of new vocabulary and carefully introduces new words, new meanings of familiar words, and idioms. New subject-specific terms are bold-faced and included in the Glossary.
- **Background knowledge:** The text assumes little prior knowledge and anchors the reader using familiar examples and analogies.
- **Sentence structure:** The text uses simple sentence structures whenever possible, but where complex sentences are needed to clarify links between ideas, the structures used are those which research has shown to enhance comprehension.

For More Information

To find out more about Start-to-Finish Core Content, visit www.donjohnston.com for full product information, standards and research base.